Project 2025: Heritage Foundation's Vision

A Guide to the Conservative Blueprint for Change

Cameron J. Blake

Copyright © 2024 Cameron J. Blake

All rights reserved.

No part of this book may be reproduced, distributed, or transmitted in any form or by any means, including photocopying, recording, or other electronic or mechanical methods, without the prior written permission of the publisher, except in the case of brief quotations embodied in critical reviews and certain other noncommercial uses permitted by copyright law. For permission requests, please contact the publisher.

Table of Contents

Introduction...5
Chapter 1: Introduction to Project 2025...........10
   Overview of the Heritage Foundation and Its Mission 12
   Importance of the Project 2025 Initiative........................ 13
   Goals and Objectives of the Book.............................14
Chapter 2: The Conservative Movement: A Historical Perspective...16
   Origins of the Conservative Movement in America..16
   Key Figures and Milestones...................................... 18
   Evolution of Conservative Thought...........................19
Chapter 3: Core Principles of Conservatism.....22
   Explanation of Fundamental Conservative Values.. 22
   The Role of Individual Liberty, Limited Government, and Free Markets..23
   How These Principles Inform Policy-Making...........25
Chapter 4: Policy Framework for Change........ 28
   Overview of the Major Policy Areas Addressed in Project 2025... 28
   Strategies for Implementation..30
   Case Studies of Successful Conservative Policies......31
Chapter 5: Economic Vision: Building Prosperity 34
   Conservative Approaches to Economic Growth and Job Creation... 34
   Tax Reform, Deregulation, and Trade Policy........... 36
   The Importance of Fiscal Responsibility................... 38
Chapter 6: National Security and Foreign Policy.. 40

Conservative Perspectives on National Defense...... 40
Strategies for Strengthening U.S. Military and Alliances...............41
The Role of America in Global Affairs............ 43

Chapter 7: Education Reform: A New Approach.. 46

Examination of the Current Education System........46
Conservative Solutions for Improving Educational Outcomes................47
The Role of School Choice and Parental Empowerment................49

Chapter 8: Healthcare Solutions: A Market-Driven Approach............... 52

Challenges Facing the Healthcare System...............52
Conservative Alternatives to Government-Run Healthcare............... 54
Emphasis on Competition and Innovation...............55

Chapter 9: Immigration Policy: A Conservative Framework............... 58

Understanding the Complexities of Immigration.... 58
Proposed Reforms and Enforcement Strategies...... 60
The Impact of Immigration on American Society.... 62

Chapter 10: Cultural Issues and Social Policy... 65

Conservative Values in the Context of Modern Social Issues............... 65
Strategies for Promoting Family and Community Values...............67
The Role of Faith and Tradition in Society............68

Chapter 11: Engaging the Grassroots: Building a Movement............... 71

Importance of Grassroots Activism in Achieving

Change...71
Strategies for Mobilizing Supporters and Volunteers.. 73
Case Studies of Successful Conservative Campaigns 74
Chapter 12: The Road Ahead: Implementing the Vision...77
Action Steps for Policymakers and Citizens...............77
The Importance of Staying Engaged and Informed. 79
Closing Thoughts on the Future of Conservatism in America.. 80
Conclusion..82

Introduction

In a time marked by profound change and shifting political landscapes, the call for a coherent and principled vision for America's future has never been more urgent. "Project 2025: Heritage Foundation's Vision" presents a timely blueprint that articulates a conservative framework for change, aiming to resonate not only with dedicated conservatives but also with all those who cherish liberty, individual rights, and a flourishing society.

At its core, this book serves as a guide to understanding the key principles and policies that will shape a revitalized conservative agenda. The Heritage Foundation, a cornerstone of conservative thought, has long been a beacon for those advocating for limited government, free markets, and traditional values. "Project 2025" represents a comprehensive effort to provide actionable strategies and ideas that can restore confidence in American institutions and invigorate the conservative movement.

The political climate today is rife with polarization and discontent. Many Americans feel disillusioned by the status quo, questioning whether their voices truly matter in shaping the nation's future. This book seeks to address those concerns by presenting a coherent vision that prioritizes the values and ideals that have historically defined American conservatism. It offers a pathway not only for conservatives but for anyone committed to ensuring a prosperous and secure future for the United States.

Understanding the historical context of the conservative movement is crucial for grasping the relevance of Project 2025. The conservative ideology has evolved significantly since its inception, shaped by key figures and pivotal moments that reflect the changing needs and challenges of society. From the foundational principles laid out by thinkers such as Edmund Burke and William F. Buckley Jr. to contemporary leaders who advocate for robust policies, the conservative narrative is rich and multifaceted. Recognizing this legacy helps frame the current dialogue and positions Project 2025 within a larger continuum of thought and action.

Central to this vision are the core principles of conservatism—individual liberty, personal responsibility, and the belief in a limited, accountable government. These tenets serve as guiding lights for the policies proposed throughout this book. They reflect a commitment to empowering individuals rather than relying solely on government solutions. In this framework, citizens are viewed as active participants in their own lives, equipped to pursue their aspirations and contribute to their communities.

The landscape of public policy presents a complex tapestry of issues, each deserving of careful consideration and strategic response. Project 2025 examines critical areas including the economy, education, healthcare, immigration, and national security, proposing innovative approaches rooted in conservative values. Each chapter of this book offers a detailed exploration of these policy domains, outlining the challenges faced and the strategies that can be employed to address them effectively.

In the realm of economics, the focus is on fostering growth and opportunity through prudent fiscal management, regulatory reform, and a commitment to free markets. History has demonstrated that when individuals and businesses are unencumbered by excessive regulation and taxation, innovation flourishes, and prosperity follows. The discussion here will highlight successful examples of economic policy that can be replicated to revitalize American prosperity.

National security is another paramount concern in today's world. As global threats evolve, so too must America's strategies for defense and diplomacy. Project 2025 advocates for a robust military posture, coupled with smart, principled foreign policy that reflects America's values while safeguarding its interests. This dual approach recognizes that security cannot be achieved solely through military might; it requires a thoughtful engagement with allies and a clear-eyed assessment of adversaries.

Education reform emerges as a critical element in shaping the future of the nation. A strong education system is essential for nurturing informed and engaged citizens capable of navigating the complexities of modern society. The book outlines conservative solutions that prioritize choice, accountability, and innovation, ensuring that all students have access to quality education that equips them for success.

Healthcare, too, remains a pressing issue. Many Americans are dissatisfied with the current system, which is often characterized by rising costs and limited choices. Project 2025 offers market-driven alternatives that seek to empower patients and providers alike, fostering a healthcare landscape where competition and transparency lead to better outcomes for all.

Immigration policy is yet another area ripe for thoughtful reform. Balancing compassion with security is a delicate task that requires a nuanced approach. The book will explore conservative perspectives that advocate for effective enforcement of immigration laws while also recognizing the contributions that immigrants make to American society.

Cultural issues, often divisive in today's discourse, will be examined through the lens of conservative values. The book seeks to articulate a vision that honors tradition while addressing contemporary challenges. The importance of community, family, and faith will be highlighted as foundational elements that contribute to a healthy society.

Engagement with grassroots movements is vital for the success of any policy initiative. Project 2025 emphasizes the need for mobilizing citizens at the local level, fostering a sense of ownership and participation in the political process. By empowering individuals and communities, conservatives can create a robust movement capable of driving meaningful change.

As the final chapters unfold, readers will find practical recommendations for implementing the vision laid out in this book. The path to a renewed conservative agenda is not merely about ideas; it is about action. Each policy recommendation is crafted to be actionable, providing a roadmap for policymakers, activists, and concerned citizens alike.

"Project 2025: Heritage Foundation's Vision" is more than a call to action; it is a comprehensive framework for understanding the challenges and opportunities that lie ahead. By embracing the core principles of conservatism and committing to a proactive agenda, we can ensure a future that honors our past while boldly addressing the needs of our time. The vision presented here is one of hope, grounded in the belief that America's best days are yet to come—if we choose to engage with purpose and conviction.

Chapter 1: Introduction to Project 2025

In the midst of an era characterized by rapid change and heightened political division, the need for a clear and actionable vision for America's future is undeniable. "Project 2025" emerges from the esteemed Heritage Foundation, a leading conservative think tank with a rich history of advocating for principles that uphold individual liberty, free enterprise, and limited government. This chapter serves as a foundational introduction, outlining the Heritage Foundation's mission and the significance of the Project 2025 initiative. Readers will gain insight into the book's goals and objectives, laying the groundwork for a thorough understanding of the conservative blueprint for change.

As the political landscape evolves, the Heritage Foundation remains steadfast in its commitment to shaping policy through rigorous research and advocacy. Established in 1973, the Foundation has become a preeminent voice for conservative thought, engaging policymakers, scholars, and citizens alike. With an emphasis on promoting the ideas that underpin a free society, the Foundation's work spans a wide range of issues—from economic policy to national security, education reform, and cultural conservatism. Project 2025 represents a bold initiative to synthesize these ideas into a coherent strategy that addresses the challenges facing America today.

The importance of the Project 2025 initiative cannot be overstated. As Americans grapple with pressing issues—ranging from economic uncertainty to national security threats—the need for a unified, principled response is more critical than ever. Project 2025 aims to not only articulate a conservative vision but also to provide actionable strategies for implementation. This book seeks to empower readers with the knowledge and tools necessary to engage in the political process, fostering a sense of agency and responsibility that is essential for a vibrant democracy.

The goals and objectives of this book are clear: to inform, inspire, and mobilize. By unpacking the key tenets of the conservative agenda, this book aims to reach a diverse audience, encouraging thoughtful dialogue and informed action. Readers will come away with a comprehensive understanding of the principles that underpin conservatism, as well as practical steps for promoting these ideas within their communities and at the national level.

Overview of the Heritage Foundation and Its Mission

The Heritage Foundation has played a pivotal role in the development and articulation of conservative policies over the past several decades. Founded by a group of scholars and activists who sought to promote conservative ideas in a post-Vietnam War America, the Foundation was built on the belief that free societies thrive when individuals are empowered to make choices that affect their lives. Its mission is to formulate and promote public policies based on the principles of free enterprise, limited government, individual freedom, traditional American values, and a strong national defense.

The Foundation has become known for its rigorous research and its ability to influence public policy at both state and federal levels. Through publications, expert testimony, and direct engagement with policymakers, the Heritage Foundation seeks to provide the intellectual ammunition necessary for conservatives to advance their agenda. Its research is grounded in the belief that policies should be designed to promote human flourishing and the common good, while respecting the dignity and rights of every individual.

Moreover, the Heritage Foundation recognizes the importance of grassroots engagement in achieving its mission. It actively seeks to empower citizens by providing them with the tools and information needed to advocate for conservative principles within their communities. This commitment to public engagement underscores the Foundation's belief that a vibrant democracy requires active participation from informed citizens.

Importance of the Project 2025 Initiative

Project 2025 stands out as a significant undertaking within the Heritage Foundation's broader mission. Launched in response to the complex challenges facing America today, the initiative aims to create a comprehensive and actionable framework for conservatives seeking to enact meaningful change. The urgency of this project arises from the recognition that, as the nation faces economic instability, cultural upheaval, and security threats, a clear vision for the future is essential.

The importance of Project 2025 lies not only in its ambitious scope but also in its potential to galvanize a diverse coalition of supporters. By articulating a vision that resonates with traditional conservative values while addressing contemporary challenges, the initiative seeks to broaden the appeal of conservatism. It aims to attract not only seasoned conservatives but also those who may be disillusioned by the current political climate, offering them a pathway to engage in the political process.

Additionally, Project 2025 emphasizes the importance of practical solutions. It recognizes that while ideas are important, their true value lies in their implementation. By focusing on actionable policies and strategies, the initiative seeks to bridge the gap between conservative ideals and real-world outcomes. This practical approach is designed to inspire confidence among citizens and policymakers alike, reinforcing the belief that meaningful change is possible.

Goals and Objectives of the Book

The goals of "Project 2025: Heritage Foundation's Vision" are multifaceted, encompassing education, engagement, and empowerment. At its core, the book aims to inform readers about the key principles of conservatism and the specific policies that can lead to a prosperous and secure America. It seeks to break down complex issues into digestible insights, making the content accessible to a broad audience.

Another crucial objective is to inspire action. The book will not only present challenges but will also offer solutions, equipping readers with the knowledge needed to advocate for change in their communities. By highlighting successful case studies and best practices, it aims to motivate citizens to become active participants in the political process, whether through grassroots activism, policy advocacy, or informed voting.

Finally, the book aspires to create a sense of community among its readers. By fostering dialogue around shared values and common goals, it seeks to cultivate a network of engaged citizens committed to the conservative agenda. This sense of belonging is vital for building a robust movement capable of influencing public policy and shaping the future of America.

Chapter 1 serves as a foundational introduction to the Heritage Foundation and the significance of Project 2025. It outlines the organization's mission, the importance of the initiative, and the book's goals and objectives. As readers progress through the subsequent chapters, they will gain a deeper understanding of the conservative principles that underpin this vision, along with practical strategies for bringing about meaningful change in their communities and beyond.

Chapter 2: The Conservative Movement: A Historical Perspective

To fully appreciate the vision laid out in "Project 2025," it is essential to understand the historical roots of the conservative movement in America. This chapter delves into the origins of conservatism, highlighting key figures and milestones that have shaped its trajectory. It will also examine the evolution of conservative thought, providing context for the principles that underpin contemporary conservative policies. By tracing the development of the movement, readers will gain insight into its foundational beliefs and how they have adapted to meet the challenges of changing times.

Origins of the Conservative Movement in America

The conservative movement in America can trace its origins back to the late 18th century, rooted in the principles enshrined in the Constitution and the Bill of Rights. The framers of the Constitution, including figures like James Madison and Alexander Hamilton, emphasized the importance of limited government, individual rights, and the rule of law. These foundational ideas became the bedrock of American conservatism, advocating for a government that serves the people without overstepping its bounds.

However, the modern conservative movement as we recognize it today began to coalesce in the aftermath of World War II. The geopolitical landscape had shifted dramatically, and the rise of the Soviet Union as a global superpower created a sense of urgency among those who believed in the principles of capitalism and democracy. The failure of the New Deal and the perceived excesses of the Great Society initiatives further fueled discontent among many Americans who felt that government intervention was undermining individual freedoms and stifling economic growth.

The publication of influential works, such as William F. Buckley Jr.'s "God and Man at Yale" in 1951, helped galvanize the movement by critiquing liberal orthodoxy and advocating for a return to traditional values. This era also saw the establishment of the National Review, a magazine dedicated to promoting conservative thought and providing a platform for intellectual discourse. Buckley and others sought to unify various strands of conservatism—fiscal conservatism, social conservatism, and foreign policy hawkishness—into a cohesive movement.

Key Figures and Milestones

Several key figures emerged during this formative period, each contributing to the development of conservative ideology and strategy. Ronald Reagan, for instance, would become one of the most emblematic figures of the movement, combining charismatic leadership with a compelling vision of a prosperous America rooted in free markets and limited government. His election as president in 1980 marked a significant milestone for conservatives, signaling a shift in the political landscape.

Other influential figures included Barry Goldwater, whose candidacy in 1964 helped lay the groundwork for the modern conservative coalition. Goldwater's staunch advocacy for limited government and individual liberties resonated with many disenchanted with the liberal policies of the time. His campaign, though unsuccessful, energized grassroots activists and signaled a departure from the moderate Republicanism that had dominated the party.

The emergence of the religious right in the late 1970s further transformed the conservative movement. Leaders such as Jerry Falwell and Pat Robertson mobilized evangelical Christians to engage in the political process, emphasizing issues like abortion and traditional family values. This coalition expanded the base of the conservative movement and solidified the

Republican Party's identity as the primary vehicle for conservative activism.

Evolution of Conservative Thought

As the conservative movement matured, it underwent significant evolution in response to changing social, economic, and political landscapes. The late 20th century brought about new challenges, including globalization, technological advancements, and cultural shifts. Conservatives had to adapt their strategies and policies to address these developments while remaining true to their foundational principles.

The 1990s saw the rise of "compassionate conservatism," championed by figures like George W. Bush. This approach sought to reconcile traditional conservative values with a focus on social issues, advocating for policies aimed at reducing poverty and improving education while maintaining a commitment to free-market principles. The idea was to broaden the appeal of conservatism by demonstrating its relevance to a wider audience.

However, the emergence of the Tea Party movement in the wake of the 2008 financial crisis signaled a renewed focus on limited government and fiscal responsibility. This grassroots movement mobilized millions of Americans who were frustrated by what they perceived as excessive government intervention and spending. It brought issues such as tax reform and entitlement reform to the forefront of the conservative agenda, influencing the Republican Party's platform in subsequent elections.

The election of Donald Trump in 2016 marked another pivotal moment in the evolution of conservatism. Trump's populist message and unorthodox style resonated with many voters who felt alienated by traditional political elites. His administration shifted the focus of the conservative movement toward nationalism and a more aggressive stance on immigration and trade. This evolution has sparked debates within the movement about the direction it should take, particularly as it grapples with the complexities of a rapidly changing world.

Understanding the historical perspective of the conservative movement is crucial for contextualizing the vision presented in Project 2025. The movement's origins in the founding principles of America, its key figures, and milestones provide a rich tapestry of ideas and strategies that have shaped its development over time. As conservatives look to the future, they must draw on this legacy while remaining adaptable to the evolving challenges that lie ahead.

In the subsequent chapters, this book will explore how these historical insights inform contemporary conservative policies and initiatives. By examining the past, readers will be better equipped to engage with the present and contribute to the ongoing dialogue about the future of conservatism in America.

Chapter 3: Core Principles of Conservatism

The conservative movement is anchored in a set of core principles that define its identity and guide its policy-making. Understanding these fundamental values is essential for anyone looking to grasp the nuances of conservatism and its approach to governance. This chapter will provide an overview of these principles, focusing on individual liberty, limited government, and free markets. It will also explore how these foundational beliefs inform policy-making, offering a clear framework for the conservative vision of a thriving society.

Explanation of Fundamental Conservative Values

At the heart of conservatism lies a deep commitment to the dignity of the individual and the belief that people are best positioned to make decisions about their own lives. This perspective fosters an ethos of personal responsibility, emphasizing that individuals should be accountable for their actions and decisions. Conservatives argue that a society that encourages personal initiative and self-reliance cultivates a vibrant, dynamic culture where innovation and creativity can flourish.

Another foundational value is the importance of tradition and continuity. Conservatives believe that the wisdom of the past should inform present decisions. This respect for tradition underscores the significance of cultural norms and institutions that have stood the test of time, such as family, community, and faith. By valuing these institutions, conservatives contend that society can maintain social cohesion and stability, allowing individuals to thrive within a framework of shared values.

Additionally, the principle of a moral order is central to conservative thought. Conservatives assert that there are objective truths and moral standards that guide human behavior. This belief in an inherent moral framework informs many conservative positions on social issues, emphasizing the importance of virtue, integrity, and accountability in both personal and public life.

The Role of Individual Liberty, Limited Government, and Free Markets

Individual liberty is arguably the cornerstone of conservative philosophy. The belief that every person has the right to pursue their own happiness, make their own choices, and enjoy the fruits of their labor is a driving force behind conservative policy. This emphasis on freedom extends to economic, social, and political realms, advocating for a society where individuals are empowered to chart their own course without undue interference from the state.

Limited government complements the principle of individual liberty. Conservatives argue that government should exist to protect the rights of its citizens, not to dictate how they live their lives. A government constrained by the rule of law is seen as essential to safeguarding freedom and ensuring that power is not concentrated in the hands of a few. This belief fosters skepticism toward expansive government programs and interventions, as conservatives contend that these often lead to unintended consequences and an erosion of personal freedoms.

Free markets play a crucial role in the conservative vision of a prosperous society. The belief in capitalism as the most effective means of creating wealth and opportunity is deeply rooted in conservative thought. Free markets encourage competition, drive innovation, and provide consumers with choices, all of which contribute to economic growth. Conservatives argue that when individuals are free to pursue their economic interests, the benefits extend to society as a whole, lifting people out of poverty and improving living standards.

How These Principles Inform Policy-Making

The core principles of conservatism provide a framework for policy-making that prioritizes individual empowerment, economic freedom, and societal stability. These principles inform conservative positions on a wide range of issues, from taxation and healthcare to education and national security.

In the realm of taxation, conservatives advocate for lower taxes and simplified tax codes, believing that individuals should retain more of their earnings to invest in their own futures. This approach aligns with the principle of individual liberty, allowing citizens to allocate resources as they see fit, rather than entrusting the government to make those decisions for them.

When it comes to healthcare, conservatives often emphasize market-based solutions that encourage competition and innovation. The belief that individuals should have the freedom to choose their healthcare providers and plans reflects a commitment to personal responsibility and autonomy. Rather than relying on government-run healthcare systems, conservatives argue for reforms that empower patients and providers, fostering an environment where quality care can thrive.

In education, the conservative approach centers around school choice, advocating for options such as charter schools, vouchers, and homeschooling. This perspective aligns with the principle of individual liberty, enabling families to select educational pathways that best suit their children's needs. Conservatives believe that by introducing competition into the education system, overall quality can improve, benefitting students and families alike.

National security policy is also heavily influenced by conservative principles. The commitment to a strong national defense stems from the belief that a secure nation is essential for preserving individual freedoms. Conservatives advocate for robust military funding and a proactive approach to foreign policy, emphasizing the need to protect American interests and uphold global stability.

The core principles of conservatism—individual liberty, limited government, and free markets—form the foundation of a coherent and compelling vision for governance. These values are not only theoretical; they inform practical policy-making across various domains. By grounding their approaches in these principles, conservatives seek to create a society where individuals are empowered, economies flourish, and communities thrive.

As we move forward in this book, it will be essential to keep these foundational principles in mind. Each subsequent chapter will build on this understanding, examining how these values manifest in specific policy areas and providing actionable insights for engaging with the conservative agenda. Through this exploration, readers will gain a deeper appreciation for the conservative vision of a prosperous and free society.

Chapter 4: Policy Framework for Change

As the conservative movement seeks to address the pressing challenges facing America today, a coherent policy framework becomes essential. "Project 2025" outlines key areas where conservative principles can be effectively translated into actionable strategies that promote individual liberty, economic growth, and societal well-being. This chapter will provide an overview of the major policy areas addressed in Project 2025, outline strategies for implementation, and present case studies of successful conservative policies that exemplify these approaches.

Overview of the Major Policy Areas Addressed in Project 2025

Project 2025 encompasses a broad spectrum of policy areas critical to shaping a conservative agenda for the future. These include:

1. Economic Policy: Focusing on tax reform, regulatory relief, and promoting free markets to stimulate growth and innovation.

2. Healthcare: Advocating for market-driven healthcare solutions that enhance patient choice and reduce costs.

3. Education: Emphasizing school choice and parental empowerment to improve educational outcomes and foster accountability.

4. National Security: Strengthening military capabilities and asserting American interests abroad to ensure national safety and global stability.

5. Immigration: Pursuing reforms that balance security with compassion, advocating for effective enforcement while recognizing the contributions of immigrants.

6. Cultural and Social Issues: Promoting traditional values, family structures, and community engagement to strengthen societal foundations.

7. Judicial Appointments: Ensuring that the judiciary reflects constitutional values, focusing on the appointment of judges who uphold the rule of law and protect individual rights.

8. Environmental Policy: Advocating for responsible stewardship of natural resources through free-market solutions rather than excessive regulation.

By addressing these policy areas, Project 2025 aims to provide a comprehensive conservative agenda that resonates with the needs and concerns of Americans across the political spectrum.

Strategies for Implementation

The successful implementation of conservative policies requires a multifaceted approach that engages a wide array of stakeholders. Here are some key strategies for putting the Project 2025 agenda into action:

1. Grassroots Mobilization: Building a robust grassroots network is essential for amplifying the conservative message. Engaging citizens through local organizations, town halls, and community events can foster a sense of ownership and empower individuals to advocate for policy changes.

2. Policy Advocacy and Education: Creating educational materials and resources that explain conservative policies and their benefits can help demystify complex issues. This includes leveraging digital platforms and social media to reach a broader audience and engage in constructive dialogue.

3. Collaboration with Stakeholders: Building coalitions with business leaders, community organizations, and other interest groups can strengthen the conservative agenda. Collaborative efforts can lead to more comprehensive solutions and enhance the credibility of policy proposals.

4. Targeted Legislative Efforts: Identifying key legislative opportunities at both the state and federal levels is

critical for advancing the conservative agenda. This includes working with elected officials to draft and promote legislation that aligns with Project 2025's objectives.

5. Utilizing Research and Data: Grounding policy proposals in rigorous research and data analysis enhances their credibility. By showcasing successful case studies and evidence-based outcomes, conservatives can make a compelling case for their initiatives.

Case Studies of Successful Conservative Policies

Examining successful conservative policies provides valuable insights into the effectiveness of the principles outlined in Project 2025. Here are a few notable case studies:

1. Tax Reform in the 1980s: The Tax Reform Act of 1986, championed by President Ronald Reagan, significantly simplified the tax code and lowered tax rates. By broadening the tax base and eliminating many loopholes, the reform stimulated economic growth and set a precedent for future tax policy. The principles of lower taxes and reduced regulation laid the groundwork for a more vibrant economy.

2. Welfare Reform of the 1990s: The Personal Responsibility and Work Opportunity Reconciliation Act of 1996 reformed the welfare system by emphasizing work requirements and state flexibility. This legislation helped reduce dependency on government assistance, encouraging personal responsibility and economic participation. By focusing on empowering individuals rather than perpetuating cycles of dependency, the reform aligned with core conservative values.

3. School Choice Initiatives: States like Florida have successfully implemented school choice policies, allowing parents to select educational options that best suit their children's needs. Programs such as vouchers and charter schools have expanded access to quality education, resulting in improved student outcomes. These initiatives demonstrate how conservative principles can lead to practical solutions that enhance educational opportunities.

4. Energy Deregulation: Texas's deregulation of its electricity market in the early 2000s serves as a case study in the benefits of free-market principles. By allowing competition among energy providers, Texas has seen lower electricity prices and increased innovation in energy generation, including a significant investment in renewable sources. This example illustrates how deregulation can foster a more efficient and consumer-friendly market.

5. **Community Policing Strategies:** Conservative approaches to crime prevention, such as community policing, emphasize collaboration between law enforcement and local communities. Programs that prioritize building trust and engagement have led to reductions in crime rates in several cities, demonstrating the effectiveness of conservative strategies in enhancing public safety while respecting individual rights.

The policy framework outlined in Project 2025 is built on a comprehensive understanding of the challenges facing America today and the conservative principles that can guide effective solutions. By addressing key policy areas and employing targeted strategies for implementation, conservatives can advocate for meaningful change that resonates with citizens across the country.

The successful case studies presented here illustrate the potential of conservative policies to drive positive outcomes, reinforcing the belief that a principled approach to governance can lead to prosperity and security. As we move forward in this book, it will be important to keep these examples in mind, as they offer valuable lessons and inspiration for the ongoing conservative agenda. Each subsequent chapter will delve deeper into specific policy areas, providing actionable insights and recommendations to further the vision of Project 2025.

Chapter 5: Economic Vision: Building Prosperity

A robust economy is the cornerstone of a prosperous society, and conservatives believe that economic growth and job creation are best achieved through principles that empower individuals and businesses. This chapter explores the conservative approaches to economic growth, emphasizing the importance of tax reform, deregulation, and trade policy. Additionally, it highlights the necessity of fiscal responsibility as a guiding principle for sustainable economic prosperity. By understanding these elements, readers will gain insight into how a conservative economic vision can drive meaningful change and improve the lives of Americans.

Conservative Approaches to Economic Growth and Job Creation

At the heart of the conservative economic agenda is the belief that a thriving economy is built on the foundations of individual initiative and free enterprise. Conservatives advocate for policies that empower entrepreneurs, encourage investment, and stimulate job creation. By fostering an environment where businesses can innovate and expand, conservatives argue that economic prosperity benefits everyone.

Key to this approach is the understanding that government does not create jobs; rather, it is the private sector that drives employment and economic activity. Conservatives assert that when individuals are free to pursue their entrepreneurial ambitions, the result is increased productivity, higher wages, and a broader tax base. This philosophy underpins the belief that a flourishing economy requires minimal interference from the government, allowing market forces to dictate outcomes.

Conservatives also recognize the importance of investing in human capital. This means promoting education and skills training to ensure that the workforce is equipped to meet the demands of a changing economy. By focusing on educational reform and vocational training, conservatives aim to prepare individuals for high-demand jobs, reducing unemployment and fostering upward mobility.

Tax Reform, Deregulation, and Trade Policy

Tax Reform

Tax policy plays a pivotal role in shaping economic growth. Conservatives advocate for a tax system that is fair, simple, and conducive to investment. This involves lowering tax rates and broadening the tax base, enabling individuals and businesses to retain more of their earnings. The belief is that when people have more disposable income, they are more likely to spend and invest, driving economic activity.

The Tax Cuts and Jobs Act of 2017 is a prime example of successful conservative tax reform. By reducing the corporate tax rate and providing tax relief for individuals, the legislation aimed to stimulate economic growth. Proponents argue that the resulting increase in business investment and job creation validates the conservative approach to taxation. This reform illustrates the potential of tax policy to catalyze economic expansion when structured with a focus on incentivizing productivity.

Deregulation

Deregulation is another cornerstone of conservative economic policy. The rationale behind deregulation is rooted in the belief that excessive government regulation stifles innovation and burdens businesses with unnecessary costs. By removing outdated and onerous regulations, conservatives aim to create an environment where entrepreneurs can thrive.

The impact of deregulation can be seen in various industries, including energy and telecommunications. For instance, the deregulation of the natural gas market in the 1980s led to increased competition, resulting in lower prices for consumers and enhanced energy security. Similarly, deregulation in the telecommunications sector spurred innovation and improved services, demonstrating how conservative policies can lead to tangible benefits for consumers and businesses alike.

Trade Policy

Conservatives also advocate for free trade as a means of fostering economic growth. By promoting open markets and reducing trade barriers, conservatives argue that countries can benefit from comparative advantages, leading to lower prices for consumers and increased competitiveness for domestic industries. Free trade agreements, such as the United States-Mexico-Canada Agreement (USMCA), exemplify this approach by facilitating trade between nations while ensuring fair competition.

However, conservatives recognize the need for fair trade practices that protect American workers and industries.

This involves addressing unfair trade practices and advocating for policies that level the playing field. By combining a commitment to free trade with a focus on fair competition, conservatives aim to create an economic environment that supports growth while safeguarding American interests.

The Importance of Fiscal Responsibility

Fiscal responsibility is a fundamental principle that underpins the conservative economic vision. Conservatives believe that a government that spends beyond its means undermines economic stability and burdens future generations with debt. Therefore, a commitment to balanced budgets and prudent fiscal management is essential for fostering long-term economic growth.

A responsible fiscal policy involves prioritizing essential services while eliminating wasteful spending. Conservatives advocate for a thorough examination of government programs to ensure that taxpayer dollars are being used effectively. By focusing on accountability and transparency, fiscal responsibility fosters public trust and ensures that resources are allocated to initiatives that yield the greatest benefit.

Moreover, maintaining a strong national debt position is vital for economic health. High levels of debt can lead to increased interest rates, limiting investment and consumption. By adhering to principles of fiscal responsibility, conservatives aim to create a stable economic environment that encourages growth and investment, ultimately benefiting all Americans.

The conservative economic vision is rooted in principles that prioritize individual empowerment, free enterprise, and fiscal responsibility. By advocating for tax reform, deregulation, and fair trade policies, conservatives seek to create an environment where businesses can thrive and job creation flourishes. The emphasis on fiscal responsibility ensures that economic growth is sustainable and benefits future generations.

As we progress through this book, the ideas presented in this chapter will serve as a foundation for understanding how conservative economic policies can lead to a prosperous and secure future. Subsequent chapters will explore specific policy areas in greater depth, providing actionable insights that align with the principles of Project 2025. By engaging with this vision, readers will be better equipped to advocate for a conservative agenda that promotes economic growth and enhances the well-being of all Americans.

Chapter 6: National Security and Foreign Policy

In an increasingly complex and interconnected world, national security and foreign policy are paramount concerns for the United States. For conservatives, a strong national defense is not merely an option; it is a fundamental obligation of the government to protect its citizens and uphold American interests abroad. This chapter explores conservative perspectives on national defense, strategies for strengthening the U.S. military and alliances, and the role of America in global affairs. Understanding these elements is crucial for comprehending the conservative vision of a secure and influential United States.

Conservative Perspectives on National Defense

Conservatives hold a steadfast belief in the necessity of a robust national defense to safeguard the nation's sovereignty and protect its citizens. This perspective is rooted in the understanding that threats to national security can arise from both state and non-state actors, requiring a comprehensive and proactive approach to defense policy.

One of the core tenets of conservative national defense policy is the commitment to maintaining military

40

superiority. Conservatives argue that a strong military deters adversaries and reassures allies. This includes investing in advanced technology, modernizing forces, and ensuring that troops are well-equipped and trained. The belief is that a formidable military presence not only protects U.S. interests but also contributes to global stability.

Moreover, conservatives emphasize the importance of preparedness and strategic foresight. This involves assessing emerging threats, whether they stem from terrorism, cyber warfare, or geopolitical rivalries, and ensuring that the military is equipped to address these challenges. The recognition that the nature of warfare is evolving necessitates a flexible and adaptive defense strategy that can respond to new realities.

Strategies for Strengthening U.S. Military and Alliances

To enhance national security, conservatives advocate for several key strategies aimed at strengthening the U.S. military and its alliances:

1. Increased Defense Spending: Conservatives typically support raising defense budgets to ensure that the military can meet its commitments both at home and abroad. Adequate funding allows for the acquisition of new technologies, personnel training, and readiness initiatives. The argument is that investing in defense not

only enhances military capabilities but also stimulates economic growth through job creation in the defense sector.

2. Modernization of Forces: As global threats evolve, so too must the U.S. military. Conservatives advocate for the modernization of military assets, including upgrading equipment and technology to maintain a competitive edge. This includes investing in cyber capabilities, advanced weaponry, and unmanned systems to address 21st-century challenges.

3. Strengthening Alliances and Partnerships: Conservatives recognize the importance of alliances in promoting national security. Strengthening relationships with NATO allies and other strategic partners is seen as essential for collective defense. Conservatives argue that fostering cooperation through joint exercises, intelligence sharing, and mutual defense commitments enhances global security while reducing the burden on American forces.

4. Strategic Deterrence: A conservative approach to national security emphasizes deterrence as a primary strategy. By clearly communicating the consequences of aggression, the U.S. can dissuade potential adversaries from engaging in hostile actions. This requires not only a credible military presence but also a commitment to respond decisively to threats.

5. Promoting Regional Stability: Conservatives believe that addressing instability in key regions is vital for U.S. interests. This involves supporting allies in regions such as the Middle East and Asia, providing military aid and training to bolster their defenses, and promoting democracy and human rights as a means of fostering stability.

The Role of America in Global Affairs

The role of America in global affairs has long been a subject of debate. Conservatives generally advocate for an active and engaged U.S. presence on the world stage, guided by the principles of strength and resolve. This approach is rooted in the belief that American leadership is crucial for maintaining international order and promoting democratic values.

One key aspect of America's role in global affairs is its commitment to collective security. Conservatives argue that the U.S. should take the lead in addressing global threats, whether through military action, diplomatic engagement, or humanitarian assistance. This leadership role is seen as essential for countering authoritarian regimes and supporting allies who share American values.

Additionally, conservatives emphasize the importance of promoting free markets and economic partnerships as tools for fostering stability and prosperity. By advocating for free trade agreements and encouraging economic development in emerging markets, the U.S. can strengthen its global standing while promoting American interests.

Moreover, conservative foreign policy recognizes the necessity of strategic patience and pragmatism. While advocating for a strong military posture, conservatives also understand the importance of diplomacy and dialogue in resolving conflicts. This nuanced approach allows for the pursuit of American interests while maintaining the flexibility to engage with adversaries when necessary.

The conservative perspective on national security and foreign policy is rooted in a commitment to a strong military, strategic alliances, and proactive engagement in global affairs. By emphasizing the need for military superiority, modernization, and strengthened partnerships, conservatives advocate for a comprehensive approach to national defense that addresses the complexities of modern threats.

As America navigates the challenges of an evolving world, the principles outlined in this chapter will serve as a foundation for understanding the conservative vision of national security. Subsequent chapters will explore how these principles can be applied to specific policy areas, providing actionable insights for promoting a secure and prosperous future for the United States and its allies. By engaging with this vision, readers will be better equipped to advocate for a conservative agenda that prioritizes national defense and reinforces America's role as a leader on the global stage.

Chapter 7: Education Reform: A New Approach

The state of education in America has become a topic of significant concern and debate in recent years. Many citizens question whether the current education system effectively prepares students for the challenges of the modern world. Conservatives argue that the existing framework often stifles innovation, accountability, and parental involvement. This chapter examines the current education system, presents conservative solutions for improving educational outcomes, and highlights the critical role of school choice and parental empowerment in fostering a better educational environment.

Examination of the Current Education System

The current education system in the United States is characterized by a one-size-fits-all approach that often fails to meet the diverse needs of students. Public schools, particularly in urban areas, face numerous challenges, including overcrowded classrooms, inadequate funding, and a lack of resources. Standardized testing and bureaucratic regulations can lead to a focus on rote learning rather than critical thinking and creativity.

Many parents express frustration over the limitations imposed by traditional public schools, particularly when their children struggle to thrive in a system that does not accommodate different learning styles or paces. Moreover, issues such as declining academic performance, particularly in key areas like mathematics and reading, raise concerns about whether the current education system is adequately preparing students for future success.

The COVID-19 pandemic further highlighted these systemic issues, exposing gaps in learning and access to technology. As schools transitioned to remote learning, many students faced significant setbacks, particularly those from lower-income families who lacked access to necessary resources. The pandemic underscored the urgent need for a reevaluation of the education system and a shift toward solutions that prioritize student outcomes and parental involvement.

Conservative Solutions for Improving Educational Outcomes

Conservatives advocate for a range of solutions aimed at improving educational outcomes and ensuring that all students receive a quality education. These solutions are grounded in the belief that educational success stems from increased accountability, competition, and innovation.

1. Accountability in Education: Conservatives emphasize the importance of accountability measures to ensure that schools are held responsible for student performance. This includes implementing transparent metrics for evaluating school effectiveness, such as student achievement scores and graduation rates. By holding schools accountable, parents and communities can better assess the quality of education their children receive and advocate for necessary improvements.

2. Decentralized Decision-Making: Moving decision-making power away from centralized bureaucracies and into the hands of local educators, parents, and communities can lead to more responsive and effective educational policies. Conservatives argue that local control allows for tailored approaches that meet the unique needs of students and families, fostering a culture of innovation and adaptability within schools.

3. Increased Funding for Alternative Education: To address the shortcomings of traditional public schools, conservatives support increased funding for alternative education models, including charter schools, vocational training, and online learning programs. These alternatives can provide students with diverse pathways to success, allowing them to pursue their interests and strengths in a more personalized manner.

4. Focus on Early Childhood Education: Conservatives recognize the importance of early childhood education in

laying the foundation for lifelong learning. By investing in quality pre-K programs and supporting families in their educational choices, conservatives aim to ensure that all children enter kindergarten prepared to succeed. This approach aligns with the belief that the earlier students receive support, the better their long-term educational outcomes.

The Role of School Choice and Parental Empowerment

Central to the conservative vision for education reform is the concept of school choice. Conservatives argue that parents should have the freedom to select the educational environment that best meets their children's needs, whether that be traditional public schools, charter schools, private institutions, or homeschooling.

1. Empowering Parents: School choice empowers parents to take an active role in their children's education. By providing them with the ability to choose, parents can advocate for their children's specific needs and ensure they receive the best educational experience possible. This empowerment fosters greater parental involvement, which has been shown to positively impact student achievement.

2. Competition and Innovation: Allowing for school choice creates a competitive environment where schools

must strive for excellence to attract students. This competition encourages innovation and improvement, as schools adopt best practices and tailor their offerings to meet the needs of families. In regions where school choice has been implemented, studies have shown improvements in student performance and satisfaction among parents.

3. Vouchers and Education Savings Accounts: Conservative proposals often include initiatives such as school vouchers and education savings accounts (ESAs), which provide parents with financial resources to choose the best educational options for their children. Vouchers allow families to use public funding for private school tuition, while ESAs enable families to allocate education funds for various educational expenses, including tutoring, online courses, and special programs. These initiatives can significantly enhance educational access and flexibility.

Education reform is a pressing issue that requires innovative solutions and a commitment to improving outcomes for all students. Conservatives believe that a reevaluation of the current education system is essential, advocating for accountability, local control, and increased funding for alternative education models. Central to this vision is the principle of school choice, which empowers parents and fosters a competitive environment that prioritizes student success.

As this chapter illustrates, conservative approaches to education reform have the potential to transform the educational landscape, ensuring that all children have access to quality education tailored to their unique needs. Subsequent chapters will explore specific policy initiatives and successful case studies that exemplify the principles discussed here, providing actionable insights for advancing the conservative education agenda. By engaging with these ideas, readers will be better equipped to advocate for meaningful change in the American education system.

Chapter 8: Healthcare Solutions: A Market-Driven Approach

The healthcare system in the United States faces significant challenges that impact the quality of care, access, and affordability for millions of Americans. Conservatives argue that a market-driven approach is essential for addressing these issues, advocating for solutions that prioritize competition and innovation rather than relying on government-run programs. This chapter explores the challenges confronting the healthcare system, presents conservative alternatives to government intervention, and emphasizes the importance of fostering a competitive environment to drive improvements in care delivery.

Challenges Facing the Healthcare System

The U.S. healthcare system grapples with a myriad of challenges that contribute to rising costs and uneven access to care. Some of the most pressing issues include:

1. High Costs: Healthcare spending in the United States is among the highest in the world, often leading to exorbitant costs for individuals and families. High premiums, deductibles, and out-of-pocket expenses can

deter patients from seeking necessary care, resulting in worse health outcomes.

2. Access to Care: Despite advancements in medical technology and treatment options, many Americans still face barriers to accessing healthcare services. Geographic disparities, particularly in rural areas, and a shortage of healthcare providers can limit options for patients seeking care.

3. Complexity of the System: The U.S. healthcare system is notoriously complex, with a myriad of insurance plans, providers, and regulations that can confuse patients. This complexity can lead to inefficiencies and a lack of transparency regarding costs and quality of care.

4. Government Intervention: The expansion of government involvement in healthcare, particularly through programs like Medicare and Medicaid, has contributed to rising costs and inefficiencies. Critics argue that bureaucratic regulations stifle innovation and limit choices for patients.

5. Quality of Care: While many healthcare providers offer excellent services, variability in quality can be a significant concern. Patients often struggle to assess the quality of care they are receiving, leading to questions about the value of their healthcare expenditures.

Conservative Alternatives to Government-Run Healthcare

In response to these challenges, conservatives advocate for a range of market-driven alternatives to government-run healthcare programs. These solutions are designed to enhance patient choice, reduce costs, and improve the overall quality of care.

1. Health Savings Accounts (HSAs): HSAs empower individuals to save money tax-free for medical expenses, providing greater control over their healthcare spending. By allowing patients to use their own funds for routine care, HSAs encourage responsible spending and incentivize price transparency among healthcare providers.

2. Expanded Access to Telemedicine: The rise of telemedicine offers a practical solution to improve access to care, particularly in underserved areas. Conservatives advocate for policies that eliminate regulatory barriers to telehealth services, enabling patients to receive care from providers remotely. This approach can enhance access and convenience while reducing costs.

3. Deregulation of Insurance Markets: Conservatives argue that deregulating insurance markets can foster competition and lower premiums. Allowing insurers to offer plans across state lines increases consumer choice and encourages innovation in insurance products. This

competitive environment can lead to more affordable options for consumers.

4. Value-Based Care Models: Shifting from fee-for-service models to value-based care emphasizes quality over quantity in healthcare delivery. Conservatives support initiatives that reward providers for delivering high-quality care and improving patient outcomes, aligning incentives with the best interests of patients.

5. Public-Private Partnerships: Conservatives advocate for collaboration between the public and private sectors to address healthcare challenges. By leveraging the strengths of both sectors, such partnerships can drive innovation, improve access, and enhance the quality of care while maintaining a market-driven approach.

Emphasis on Competition and Innovation

At the core of conservative healthcare solutions is the belief that competition and innovation are key drivers of improved care and reduced costs. By fostering a competitive environment, conservatives argue that the healthcare system can better respond to the needs of patients and encourage the development of innovative treatments and technologies.

1. Encouraging Competition: A competitive healthcare marketplace incentivizes providers to improve services, enhance patient experiences, and reduce costs. When patients have the freedom to choose their providers based on price and quality, it creates pressure on healthcare organizations to perform better.

2. Promoting Innovation: The conservative approach prioritizes innovation in medical technology and treatments as essential to advancing healthcare. By reducing regulatory barriers that can stifle research and development, the market can facilitate breakthroughs in healthcare solutions, leading to better outcomes for patients.

3. Transparency and Information Sharing: Encouraging transparency regarding pricing and quality of care empowers patients to make informed choices. Conservatives advocate for policies that require healthcare providers to disclose costs and outcomes, allowing patients to compare options and select the best care for their needs.

4. Incentivizing Preventive Care: A market-driven approach also emphasizes the importance of preventive care in reducing long-term healthcare costs. By promoting wellness programs and preventive services, conservatives aim to shift the focus from reactive to proactive healthcare, improving overall health outcomes.

The challenges facing the U.S. healthcare system require innovative and market-driven solutions that prioritize patient choice and competition. Conservatives believe that by embracing alternatives to government-run healthcare, such as health savings accounts, telemedicine, and value-based care models, the system can be transformed to enhance access, reduce costs, and improve quality.

By fostering a competitive environment and encouraging innovation, conservatives aim to create a healthcare system that empowers individuals and promotes better health outcomes. As we move forward in this book, the principles discussed in this chapter will serve as a foundation for understanding how conservative healthcare policies can effectively address the challenges confronting the system. Subsequent chapters will delve deeper into specific policy initiatives and successful case studies that exemplify these ideas, providing actionable insights for advancing the conservative healthcare agenda.

Chapter 9: Immigration Policy: A Conservative Framework

Immigration remains one of the most contentious and complex issues in American politics. As the nation grapples with the challenges and opportunities presented by immigration, conservatives advocate for a balanced approach that prioritizes security, legal pathways, and the contributions of immigrants to society. This chapter delves into the complexities of immigration, outlines proposed reforms and enforcement strategies, and examines the impact of immigration on American society from a conservative perspective.

Understanding the Complexities of Immigration

The topic of immigration is multifaceted, encompassing a range of issues including legal immigration pathways, illegal immigration, refugee resettlement, and the economic implications of immigration policies. Understanding these complexities is crucial for developing effective immigration policy.

1. Legal vs. Illegal Immigration: Legal immigration provides pathways for individuals seeking to live and work in the U.S. through visas, family reunification, and

employment opportunities. In contrast, illegal immigration poses significant challenges, including concerns about border security, public safety, and the rule of law. Conservatives emphasize the importance of addressing illegal immigration while recognizing the need for a functional legal immigration system.

2. Economic Contributions: Immigrants play a vital role in the U.S. economy, contributing to various sectors, filling labor shortages, and fostering innovation. However, concerns about the impact of immigration on wages and job availability for American workers persist. Conservatives argue for policies that support legal immigration while ensuring that American workers are protected.

3. Cultural Integration: Immigration also raises questions about cultural integration and the preservation of American values. Conservatives believe that while diversity enriches society, it is essential that immigrants assimilate and embrace the principles that underpin American democracy and culture.

Proposed Reforms and Enforcement Strategies

To address the complexities of immigration, conservatives advocate for a comprehensive approach that combines reforms to the legal immigration system with robust enforcement measures to secure the borders.

1. Strengthening Border Security: A fundamental component of conservative immigration policy is the need for enhanced border security. This includes investing in physical barriers, surveillance technology, and increased personnel along the U.S.-Mexico border. By securing the border, conservatives argue that the flow of illegal immigration can be significantly reduced.

2. E-Verify Implementation: Conservatives support the widespread implementation of E-Verify, a system that allows employers to verify the employment eligibility of their workers. By mandating E-Verify for all employers, the government can discourage the hiring of illegal immigrants and promote a fair labor market for American workers.

3. Streamlining Legal Immigration: Conservatives advocate for reforms that streamline the legal immigration process. This includes reducing bureaucratic hurdles, expediting visa processing times, and expanding opportunities for high-skilled workers. By making legal immigration more accessible, the U.S. can

better meet the needs of its economy while upholding the rule of law.

4. Merit-Based Immigration: A merit-based immigration system prioritizes individuals based on skills, education, and economic contributions rather than family connections alone. Conservatives argue that this approach aligns immigration with the needs of the economy and encourages the entry of individuals who can contribute to society.

5. Addressing Asylum and Refugee Policies: Conservatives recognize the need for a fair and efficient asylum process that prioritizes genuine refugees while preventing abuse of the system. Proposed reforms include expediting claims for legitimate asylum seekers while enhancing measures to deter fraudulent applications.

The Impact of Immigration on American Society

The impact of immigration on American society is profound, influencing cultural, economic, and social dynamics. Conservatives believe that while immigration can enrich the nation, it is essential to manage it thoughtfully to maximize benefits and minimize challenges.

1. Economic Growth: Immigrants contribute significantly to economic growth, often filling vital roles in industries such as agriculture, healthcare, and technology. By addressing labor shortages and fostering innovation, immigrants enhance productivity and economic output.

2. Cultural Contributions: Immigrants bring diverse perspectives, traditions, and experiences that enrich American culture. From cuisine to art and music, these contributions enhance the social fabric of the nation. However, conservatives stress the importance of assimilation, encouraging immigrants to adopt American values and integrate into their communities.

3. Public Safety and Community Cohesion: Concerns about crime and public safety are often tied to immigration discussions. Conservatives argue that strong immigration enforcement and a focus on legal pathways enhance public safety by ensuring that

individuals entering the country are vetted and comply with the law. This approach fosters community cohesion and trust in law enforcement.

4. Political Implications: Immigration also has political implications, influencing voting patterns and the dynamics of local and national elections. Conservatives advocate for policies that promote civic engagement and encourage immigrants to embrace their role as responsible citizens.

A conservative framework for immigration policy recognizes the complexities of the issue while advocating for a balanced approach that prioritizes security, legal pathways, and the contributions of immigrants to American society. By strengthening border security, streamlining legal immigration processes, and implementing enforcement strategies, conservatives seek to create an immigration system that upholds the rule of law and supports the nation's economic and cultural vitality.

As this chapter illustrates, effective immigration policy is essential for addressing the challenges facing the U.S. While the benefits of immigration are clear, managing it thoughtfully is crucial for ensuring that it contributes positively to society. In subsequent chapters, the principles discussed here will serve as a foundation for understanding specific policy initiatives and case studies that exemplify the conservative vision for immigration reform. By engaging with these ideas, readers will be better equipped to advocate for a comprehensive immigration policy that reflects conservative values while promoting the nation's well-being.

Chapter 10: Cultural Issues and Social Policy

In an era of rapid social change and evolving cultural norms, conservative values provide a framework for understanding and addressing modern social issues. This chapter explores how these values inform responses to contemporary challenges, strategies for promoting family and community cohesion, and the vital role that faith and tradition play in shaping society. By examining these elements, we can better understand the conservative perspective on cultural issues and social policy.

Conservative Values in the Context of Modern Social Issues

Conservatives hold steadfast beliefs about the importance of family, community, and individual responsibility, which guide their responses to various social issues. In the context of modern debates surrounding topics such as marriage, education, gender identity, and personal conduct, conservative values advocate for principles that prioritize stability, integrity, and respect for tradition.

1. Family as the Fundamental Unit: Conservatives view the family as the cornerstone of a healthy society. This

belief shapes their approach to social policy, emphasizing the need to support traditional family structures. Policies that promote marriage, parenting, and family stability are seen as essential to fostering a nurturing environment for children.

2. Respect for Individual Responsibility: Individual responsibility is a key tenet of conservatism. Conservatives argue that individuals should be accountable for their choices and actions, which underpins their approach to social issues. This perspective emphasizes the importance of education, personal development, and community engagement as means to empower individuals and strengthen society.

3. Preservation of Cultural Norms: Conservative values emphasize the significance of cultural norms and traditions that have stood the test of time. Conservatives often argue that these norms provide a moral framework that guides behavior and fosters social cohesion. This perspective shapes their views on issues such as education curriculum, public policy, and community standards.

Strategies for Promoting Family and Community Values

To effectively promote family and community values, conservatives advocate for a range of strategies designed to strengthen the fabric of society.

1. Support for Family-Friendly Policies: Conservatives emphasize the importance of policies that support families, such as tax incentives for married couples, parental leave, and child care assistance. These policies are designed to alleviate the financial burdens faced by families and encourage family cohesion.

2. Community Engagement Initiatives: Encouraging community engagement and volunteerism is vital for fostering social responsibility and building connections among residents. Conservatives promote initiatives that encourage citizens to participate in local organizations, mentorship programs, and community service projects, reinforcing the importance of civic involvement.

3. Education on Family Values: Integrating discussions about family values and personal responsibility into educational curricula can help instill these principles in younger generations. Conservatives advocate for programs that teach the importance of healthy relationships, conflict resolution, and character development, laying the groundwork for responsible citizenship.

4. Promotion of Mentorship Programs: Mentorship programs can provide guidance and support to individuals, particularly youth, helping them navigate challenges and develop positive life skills. Conservatives support initiatives that connect mentors with those in need, fostering relationships that promote personal growth and accountability.

The Role of Faith and Tradition in Society

Faith and tradition play a crucial role in the conservative worldview, providing a moral compass and a sense of belonging within communities.

1. Faith as a Foundation: Many conservatives believe that faith is integral to individual and societal well-being. Religious beliefs often shape moral values, ethical conduct, and community engagement. Conservatives advocate for the protection of religious freedoms, ensuring that individuals and institutions can express their beliefs without government interference.

2. Tradition as a Guiding Principle: Conservatives emphasize the importance of traditions that promote social cohesion and continuity. These traditions can include cultural practices, family rituals, and community gatherings that reinforce shared values and foster a sense of identity. By honoring these traditions,

conservatives argue that society can maintain stability and resilience in the face of change.

3. Moral Framework for Public Policy: The influence of faith and tradition extends into public policy discussions. Conservatives argue that policies should reflect moral principles that uphold human dignity and promote the common good. This perspective often shapes conservative positions on issues such as abortion, marriage, and education.

4. Building Resilient Communities: Faith-based organizations often play a pivotal role in community service, providing support and resources to those in need. Conservatives advocate for collaboration between government and faith-based organizations to address social challenges, believing that these partnerships can effectively address issues such as poverty, addiction, and family instability.

Conservative values provide a framework for understanding and addressing modern social issues, emphasizing the importance of family, individual responsibility, and the preservation of cultural norms. Through strategies that promote family and community values, conservatives seek to strengthen the social fabric and foster a sense of belonging among citizens.

The role of faith and tradition is integral to this vision, serving as a moral compass and guiding principles that shape public policy and community engagement. As this chapter illustrates, the conservative approach to cultural issues and social policy prioritizes stability, integrity, and the well-being of individuals and families.

As we continue through this book, the principles discussed in this chapter will serve as a foundation for understanding specific policy initiatives and case studies that exemplify the conservative vision for a cohesive and thriving society. By engaging with these ideas, readers will be better equipped to advocate for policies that reflect conservative values and promote the common good.

Chapter 11: Engaging the Grassroots: Building a Movement

Grassroots activism is the backbone of any successful political movement, serving as a vital mechanism for fostering engagement, mobilizing supporters, and driving change. For conservatives, engaging the grassroots is essential not only for advancing policies but also for revitalizing the movement itself. This chapter discusses the importance of grassroots activism, outlines strategies for mobilizing supporters and volunteers, and examines case studies of successful conservative campaigns that exemplify effective grassroots engagement.

Importance of Grassroots Activism in Achieving Change

Grassroots activism embodies the principle that power lies with the people. By mobilizing individuals at the local level, grassroots movements can effectively influence public opinion, shape policy, and hold elected officials accountable. This engagement is particularly crucial in a political landscape that often feels disconnected from the concerns of everyday citizens.

1. Amplifying Voices: Grassroots activism gives individuals a platform to voice their concerns and advocate for their beliefs. This collective action amplifies the message, drawing attention to issues that may otherwise be overlooked by traditional media or political elites.

2. Building Community: Grassroots movements foster a sense of community and shared purpose among supporters. When individuals come together around common values and goals, they create networks of support that can enhance personal connections and collective action.

3. Encouraging Civic Participation: Engaging grassroots activists encourages broader civic participation, motivating individuals to become informed voters and active members of their communities. This participation is crucial for the health of democracy, as it fosters accountability and responsiveness in government.

4. Driving Electoral Success: Many successful political campaigns have demonstrated that grassroots activism is essential for electoral victories. Mobilized supporters can canvass neighborhoods, phone bank, and engage in outreach efforts that increase voter turnout and strengthen the candidate's position.

Strategies for Mobilizing Supporters and Volunteers

Effective grassroots engagement requires strategic planning and execution. Here are several key strategies for mobilizing supporters and volunteers:

1. Building a Strong Network: Establishing a robust network of supporters is essential for grassroots efforts. This can be achieved through community events, local meetings, and outreach initiatives that encourage individuals to connect with one another and share their passion for conservative values.

2. Utilizing Social Media and Technology: In the digital age, social media platforms are powerful tools for grassroots mobilization. Conservatives can leverage social media to disseminate information, organize events, and engage supporters in meaningful conversations. Technology can also facilitate online fundraising and volunteer recruitment, making it easier to reach a broader audience.

3. Training and Empowering Volunteers: Providing training and resources for volunteers is vital for ensuring their effectiveness. This includes educating them about key issues, campaign strategies, and grassroots organizing techniques. Empowered volunteers are more likely to take initiative and contribute meaningfully to the movement.

4. Fostering Local Leadership: Encouraging local leaders to emerge within the grassroots movement can enhance its sustainability and effectiveness. By identifying and supporting passionate individuals, conservatives can create a network of leaders who can mobilize their communities and drive local initiatives.

5. Establishing Clear Goals and Messaging: Successful grassroots movements have clear goals and consistent messaging that resonate with supporters. By articulating a compelling vision and emphasizing the importance of collective action, conservatives can inspire individuals to become active participants in the movement.

Case Studies of Successful Conservative Campaigns

Several case studies illustrate the power of grassroots activism in advancing conservative causes and achieving political success. These examples highlight effective strategies and the impact of engaged communities.

1. The Tea Party Movement: Emerging in 2009 in response to perceived government overreach, the Tea Party movement exemplifies the power of grassroots activism. Fueled by concerns about taxation and government spending, the movement mobilized supporters across the country, influencing the 2010

midterm elections. Through town halls, rallies, and social media, the Tea Party successfully challenged incumbents and helped elect a wave of conservative candidates to Congress, demonstrating the effectiveness of grassroots organizing.

2. The 2016 Presidential Election: Donald Trump's 2016 campaign leveraged grassroots activism to mobilize a diverse coalition of supporters. Through rallies, town halls, and a strong social media presence, the campaign engaged voters who felt disenchanted with the political establishment. The use of grassroots volunteers to canvass and engage with voters played a critical role in Trump's electoral success, showcasing how effective grassroots strategies can yield tangible results.

3. State-Level Initiatives: Grassroots efforts have also driven significant conservative policy changes at the state level. For example, the successful push for school choice initiatives in states like Florida and Arizona relied heavily on grassroots advocacy. Local organizations rallied parents, educators, and community members to advocate for legislation that expands educational options, demonstrating the power of mobilized citizens in achieving policy goals.

4. Pro-Life Movement: The pro-life movement is a long-standing example of effective grassroots activism. Organizations like the Susan B. Anthony List and local pro-life groups mobilize supporters through educational campaigns, rallies, and lobbying efforts. Their grassroots

engagement has influenced legislation at both state and federal levels, showcasing the ability of a dedicated and organized movement to effect change over time.

Engaging the grassroots is essential for building a strong conservative movement capable of driving meaningful change. By amplifying voices, fostering community, and encouraging civic participation, grassroots activism serves as a powerful force in the political landscape.

Through strategic mobilization of supporters and volunteers, conservatives can harness the energy and passion of individuals committed to their cause. The case studies presented in this chapter demonstrate the effectiveness of grassroots efforts in achieving political success and advancing conservative principles.

As we continue through this book, the strategies and insights discussed here will serve as a foundation for understanding how to engage grassroots activists effectively and build a movement that resonates with the values and aspirations of Americans. By embracing these principles, readers will be better equipped to advocate for conservative policies and inspire others to join the cause.

Chapter 12: The Road Ahead: Implementing the Vision

As we look toward the future, the implementation of the conservative vision outlined in this book requires commitment and action from both policymakers and citizens. The path ahead is filled with opportunities to promote conservative values and create meaningful change in American society. This chapter provides actionable steps for stakeholders at all levels, emphasizes the importance of remaining engaged and informed, and offers closing thoughts on the future of conservatism in America.

Action Steps for Policymakers and Citizens

1. Developing Comprehensive Policy Proposals: Policymakers should focus on developing comprehensive policy proposals that reflect the core principles of conservatism. This includes collaborating with experts, engaging with constituents, and considering the practical implications of proposed legislation. By grounding policy in research and real-world experiences, lawmakers can create initiatives that resonate with the needs of the American people.

2. Fostering Collaboration Across Levels of Government: Effective governance requires collaboration between

federal, state, and local levels. Policymakers should work together to share best practices, address challenges, and develop unified strategies for tackling pressing issues such as healthcare, education, and national security. This collaborative approach can enhance the effectiveness of conservative policies and foster a sense of shared purpose.

3. Encouraging Grassroots Engagement: Citizens play a crucial role in advocating for conservative values and holding elected officials accountable. Individuals can get involved by attending town hall meetings, participating in local advocacy groups, and engaging in grassroots campaigns. By amplifying their voices, citizens can influence public policy and ensure that their concerns are heard.

4. Utilizing Technology and Social Media: In today's digital age, technology and social media offer powerful tools for promoting conservative principles. Policymakers and activists should leverage these platforms to communicate their messages, share information, and mobilize supporters. By harnessing the reach of social media, conservatives can engage younger generations and expand their influence.

5. Investing in Education and Training: Education is key to building a strong conservative movement. Organizations should invest in training programs that equip activists and volunteers with the skills needed for effective advocacy, grassroots organizing, and public

speaking. By fostering a well-informed and capable base, conservatives can enhance their impact on policy discussions.

The Importance of Staying Engaged and Informed

The journey toward implementing the conservative vision is ongoing, and it is essential for both policymakers and citizens to remain engaged and informed. This involves:

1. Continuous Education: Staying informed about current events, policy developments, and the principles of conservatism is crucial for effective advocacy. Citizens should seek out reputable sources of information, attend lectures, and engage in discussions that deepen their understanding of the issues at hand.

2. Active Participation in the Political Process: Voting is just the beginning of civic engagement. Citizens should actively participate in the political process by attending public hearings, engaging with elected officials, and advocating for policies that align with conservative values. By remaining involved, individuals can shape the direction of their communities and the nation.

3. Building Alliances and Networks: Collaboration is vital for success. Conservatives should seek to build alliances with like-minded organizations, community

groups, and individuals. By pooling resources and sharing knowledge, these networks can amplify their collective voice and drive change more effectively.

4. Promoting Informed Debate: Engaging in constructive dialogue is essential for fostering understanding and addressing differing viewpoints. Conservatives should promote informed debate that respects diverse perspectives while articulating their own values and principles. This approach can help bridge divides and build consensus on key issues.

Closing Thoughts on the Future of Conservatism in America

The future of conservatism in America hinges on the ability of individuals and leaders to embrace the principles that have historically defined the movement while adapting to the challenges of the present and future. By staying true to the core values of individual liberty, limited government, and personal responsibility, conservatives can forge a path toward a prosperous and secure society.

As the political landscape continues to evolve, conservatism must remain relevant by addressing the concerns of everyday Americans. This requires a commitment to innovative solutions, grassroots engagement, and a focus on community building. By emphasizing the importance of family, faith, and tradition, conservatives can provide a compelling vision that resonates with citizens seeking stability and purpose in an increasingly complex world.

The road ahead is filled with opportunities for conservatives to implement their vision and make a lasting impact on American society. By taking action, remaining engaged, and fostering a spirit of collaboration, conservatives can work toward a future that honors the principles of freedom, responsibility, and opportunity for all. As we move forward, the commitment to these values will be essential for ensuring that conservatism thrives and continues to shape the future of America.

Conclusion

As we conclude "Project 2025: Heritage Foundation's Vision," it is essential to reflect on the overarching themes and principles that have been explored throughout this journey. The conservative blueprint for change articulated in this book is not merely a set of policy proposals; it is a vision rooted in the belief that individual liberty, personal responsibility, and strong communities form the foundation of a thriving society.

In the face of contemporary challenges—whether they be economic, social, or cultural—conservatives advocate for solutions that empower individuals and promote opportunity. By prioritizing economic growth through market-driven policies, supporting educational reform, and fostering a national security strategy that protects American interests, conservatives seek to create an environment where all Americans can pursue their dreams and achieve their potential.

The importance of grassroots activism cannot be overstated. Throughout this book, we have emphasized the power of engaged citizens in shaping the political landscape. Grassroots movements amplify voices, foster community, and drive change from the bottom up. As we look to the future, the commitment of individuals to remain active, informed, and involved in their communities will be crucial for advancing conservative principles and achieving meaningful policy outcomes.

Moreover, the role of faith and tradition in society serves as a guiding light for conservatives. These elements provide moral clarity and a sense of belonging, reinforcing the values that underpin a cohesive and resilient community. By promoting family, community, and civic responsibility, conservatives can nurture the social fabric that strengthens the nation.

As we navigate an ever-evolving political landscape, it is vital for conservatives to remain adaptable while staying true to their core values. Embracing innovative solutions to complex problems will be key in ensuring that the conservative movement remains relevant and effective. The commitment to fostering open dialogue, building alliances, and engaging in constructive debate will enhance our collective ability to address the pressing issues of our time.

Looking ahead to 2025 and beyond, the conservative vision outlined in this book presents a roadmap for not only policymakers but also for citizens seeking to make a difference. The principles of limited government, free markets, and personal responsibility are more than just ideals; they are practical approaches to governance that can yield positive results for all Americans.

Ultimately, the future of conservatism in America depends on the willingness of individuals to engage with these ideas and advocate for their implementation. By understanding the importance of grassroots activism, remaining informed about key issues, and fostering a spirit of community and collaboration, conservatives can work together to create a brighter future.

As we close this chapter, let us remember that the path forward is not solely about politics; it is about people—individuals, families, and communities coming together to uphold the values that have made America strong. Together, we can embrace the vision of Project 2025, champion conservative principles, and build a future that reflects our shared aspirations for a prosperous, secure, and free society.

Printed in Great Britain
by Amazon